Our Voices...

A Teen Anthology

Our Voices
Edited by Brenda's Child
Cover design by Quincy Brown
Copyright © 2008
Brenda's Child for Two-Two INK
978-0-6152-1555-6

This book is dedicated to every young person I've ever met…
You touched my life in more ways than you'll ever know.
Through you I relive my past, and anticipate a brighter future.
                                    Love Eternally,

                                    Miss Toya.
                                    A.K.A
                                    Brenda's Child

They Speak….

I AM ME

HERE WE BARE OUR SOULS

THEY CALL IT PUPPY LOVE

1. My Love
2. Gone
3. Secret Crush
4. Over You
5. Fairy Tales
6. Beautiful
7. Puppet
8. Inside
9. A Lesson
10. You are my Outlet

YOUNG WISDOM

1. Live Life to its Best
2. Something I Just Can't Handle
3. Don't Call Me Kid!
4. If You feel Pain, You're Still Alive
5. Hidden Transformation
6. Crazy Girl World
7. A Mother's Love is Great
8. Trick or Treed
9. Life is a Part of the Struggle
10. On the Street

Miss Toya

Bios

I Am Me...

Because of what you teach me,
Words you speak,
 travel deep,
in my ears
and down into my soul,
Water me with positivity,
And my confidence will grow

Self -Esteem

Please treat me well, for I am
 as I'm treated
When I am loved, I can love who I AM.
When I am cared for,
I can care for myself.
When I am treated as someone,
I can FEEL someone.

Speak to me, so I may learn to listen,
Expose the world to me,
so I may see its beauty.
Look into my eyes, so I may feel I am seen.

If you're good to me,
I can be a good person

When you smile at me, I can smile inside.
When you let me make choices,
 I know that I can choose.
When you give to me, I can give a bit back.

Touch me gently, so I may touch others.
Rest my unrest,
so that I may learn self- control,
Soothe me, so I may soothe others.

Love me, but give me room to love others.
When you treat me as successful,
 I learn to succeed.
When you respect my dreams,
I can explore reality.
When you allow my mistakes,

I can accept what they teach.

Teach me diversity of thought,
 so I may be open-minded.
Help me help others,
so I may grow to be self-less.
Demonstrate your diligence,
 so I may earn my way in life.

Show me how to laugh,
 so I may laugh with others.
Laugh at your shortcomings,
so I may accept my own.

I am someone, if I am loved.

-Lori Stephens

I AM

I am Ricardo, also known as Rico,
Puerto Rican, yes its true,
But never been to Puerto Rico.
I am talented, intelligent, tall, dark,
Handsome and cool.
But been smoking' weed, skippin' school,
Breakin' laws, actin' a fool.
I am now locked up, 17, almost, 18

There goes my Birthday, New Years,
Christmas, Thanksgiving, and Halloween.

I AM going crazy, hoping things are good
on the "Out"
Somehow I feel like my life
 is going through a drought.

I AM still Ricardo,
also known as DJ RICO,
 I will someday travel the world,
 And even go to Puerto Rico.
I AM still talented, intelligent,
tall, dark, and handsome,
I don't have a life goal yet,
but I will plan one.

I AM still locked up, and I am still 17,
 But I will get, and have a Christmas,
a Birthday, and turn 18.
On the "Out" yes, on the "Out",
It will not be on the "In"
 I will get my life together,
That's the game I want to win.

-Ricardo Navarro

ME

Strong, Black,
and independent
Talented, smart,
and self-oriented
is ME
I Strive for the best,
reach for the stars,
And always achieve my goal.

Outgoing, intellectual,
and high spirited.
Romantic, and emotional,
Inspiration gives me strength
I'll grow up to be the best,
Not like the rest.

Conservative, self-determined,
organized
Pretty, creative, and daring
Is what I'll always be.

All this comes from
how my mother raised me,
And from what GOD gave me.

-Shannan Swinton

The Years I Own

You grow up pointing fingers at everyone else,
I grew up pointing fingers at myself,
Why make them cry? Why tell all those lies?
Why let my anger control me?
Why let them kids provoke me?
I realize now, this messy life,
I made it on my own,
I hit the block, and skipped school a lot,
Fought time and time again
Been shackled up, and shown tough love,
too many times to count.
But through out it all, I stood tall,
Kept strong,

And held my dreams nice and tight,

Many sobs, and dried up tears drops,
I'm here to prove a point…
Just because you came from nothing,
Shouldn't mean you can't become something,
For in reality
you're someone's dream come true,
So don't regret or beg to redo,
For without your flaws, you wouldn't be you,
The years gone by,
I own them
They're, mine
Because without them,
 I wouldn't be here
And I wouldn't know the words that I write

-Maria Colon

Just a Girl

I am just a girl,
Who makes too many mistakes,
who can appreciate beauty,
but frowns upon fakes.
I am just a girl,
who loves what she's got,
 and is loved for who she is
 and never what she's not.

I am just a girl
who is very outspoken,
and I hold my head high,
though my heart has been broken,
I am just a girl,
who misses everyone she loves,
 and when I'm lost for answers,
I always look above.

I am just a girl
who is afraid to cry,
who is really sick of death,
since too many loved ones die.
I am just a girl
who always tries her best,
but is tired of always fighting,
and just wants to take a rest.

I am just a girl
who enjoys the finer things,
but always learns
to accept the sadness life may
bring.
I am just a girl.

-April Clark

Here We Bare Our Souls

*We get emotional,
we let it all out,
So we may let it go*

Death Ridin' Low

Death is in my hood
Everyday, and every night
Every time he rides through
Somebody else is gettin' swiped

I think I seen him before
Dressed in all black
Ridin' low through my hood
In an all black Ac'
He was creepin' up slow
Windows down
Lettin' demons go
He almost took my soul
So I had to duck down low

-Jerel Brunson

RIP Mrs.Grahm

The tears that swell within my eye
But won't dare to touch my cheek,
What is wrong with me?
Deep inside I kick and scream,
Trying so hard to fight it
And continue in pursuing my dream
How do I express?
How do I let it all go?
How do I control this…
uncontrollable anger within my soul?
It tears me to shreds,
Leaves me with baggage
that I cannot shed,
Leaves with feelings that I dread.

We were just talking over T.V. dinners,
About how much I've changed,
And I'm close to becoming a winner.
She would've been at my graduation,
If only God could have been a little
more patient.
She learned about my whole life,
In one single night.

I guess God needed his angel back home,
But why deep inside, do I feel all alone?

I've watched many people go,
It never grows old.
The feeling it provokes,
Simply no words can express,
How messed up I am in the head.
I giggle and smile,
Deep inside I know I'm in denial.
Is that not how it goes ?
No one can know,
The sorrow you hold.

- Maria Colon

Alone

Young girl in tears
 runs down the stairs
She forgets her prayers and cares
In sneakers and her underwear
And ashy knees and messed up hair
With not a penny to her name
So sick and tired of playing games
And being in and out God's favor
Fickle, fickle-loves her...hates her
And decided
if she can't save herself
She might as well just kill herself
And end the goddamned thing.

She begged for help
 and needed an angel
Needed to see life in another angle
Glasses she was looking through
were cracked
In this life she felt so trapped
Now there's nothing of her left
She's been losing sense of self
And decides if she can't save herself
She might as well just kill herself
And end the goddamned thing.

But there's just something deep
inside her
That won't let her give up
Something that still believes a door
opens
When another closes shut
She don't want all those people to
be right
When they said she'd do absolutely
nothing with her life

She just don't know where to go
from there
She got the will, ain't got the way
She flings her front door wide open
Wintertime, in sneakers and some
underwear
Struggling to breathe
Darkness creeps up all around her
She's struggling to feel and see
People call her name behind her
They're wondering what's wrong
She sighs wondering how she can
Tell the only ones that love her still
That she has HIV

- Annamarie Alleyne-Lovell

You Promised

You would be there forever!
You promised!
To never leave me
through tough times
You do so much that
I cannot say a word

All that you do touches me
To have me to a point
Where you promise
To live a normal life
I have screwed that up for you

So much that you promised
That you would always
be there for me
And never give up
That is what you do?

-Nycole Lynn Marshall Coombs

Mommy

My heart feels empty without you
You had always been there for me,
 You had always
made me feel brand new,
 That tiny heart of mine crumbled,
 The day you left me!
But I'm glad you left at peace,
with wonderful memories
So now your soul can be free.

But it really hurts
now that you're gone
 I stay up and cry,
Constantly reminiscing
 about the things we did together.
We never went through
anything negative
Mother and daughter,
I was always by your side.

We were so close,
they called us a tangle,
 Now you're looking down on me
 my guardian angel.
R.I.P Mommy
aka Two-Two.
I will always love you

-Shannan Swinton

Missing You, DAD

I have a hole in my heart
That misses you everyday
I think of you all the time
And at night I pray
Your smile is one
I'll never forget
Though it seems so long ago.

I wonder what it'd be like
 to have you here,
That sadness that I feel,
Is one I can't explain,
And even though
I try to pretend
It causes so much pain.

My life
would be so much better,
 With you here by my side,
And even though
I'm not doing good,
 I want you to know I tried.
I've tried to make you proud,
And I've tried to make you see
I might not be the greatest kid,
But I'm all that I can be.

Your patient eyes,
and gentle face,
No one can ever
Take your place
I miss you now,

my heart is sore.
As time goes by,
I miss you more.

Now you're gone,
and there's nothing I can do,
Except wait for the day,
I can finally see you.
I want you to know
that I miss you really bad,
Because I know
that you would have made...
A GREAT DAD.

-April Clark

Hole in My Heart

How do I live,
 knowing you're not here,
knowing that I need you,
 but you don't care?
I cry every night,
 not knowing why,
But tear after tear, year after year,
you're still not here.

 It's like a puzzle,
hard to put together.
I wish you were here
 and would stay forever.
I love you
because you're my dad,
but I HATE you
 because you make me feel bad.
There's a hole in my heart,
because of you,
come back into my life,
and love me too.

 I want to be Daddy's little girl,
 I want to be your whole world.
Be a dad,
and treat me like your daughter,
My life is already difficult,
please don't make it harder.
You can give me money, cars,
whatever,

but all I want is your love,
to be daddy's little girl...
all I want, is for once,
to be your whole world.

-Saphire Saez

My Heroine

She was tired of the struggle of
waking up everyday.
Sometimes she wished with the sun,
she'd be taken away.
The drugs created these horrible
thoughts in her mind,
They were able to take control of her
from time to time
She tried to do the right thing
without hurting anyone
Instead she took her own life, this is
what drugs have done

The drugs used her 'til she had
nothing left to give.
I wish I could go back and convince
her to live
My heroine who used heroin, was
important to me
Drugs don't care they can blind us
you see...
They can make you unhappy and
throw your family away
Drugs can cause great depression
and there you will stay.

-Angela Bessey

Pregnant at 14

When I was 14, I found out I was going to be mommy. I thought I had gotten the flu. At first, it started with nausea and dizziness. I was just sleeping too much and gaining weight.

When I went to the doctor, he told me, "Jacinda, it's not that your sick, you're pregnant." Suddenly, I felt shocked, and I began to cry because I was afraid of what my grandparents might think. I was young and confused, and didn't know what to do.

In the end, it turned out okay. Everyone was happy when she was born. But having a child is a scary thing; it's hard, and expensive. Sometimes I can't go out or do anything because I have a child to go home and take care of. I don't regret my daughter, but I do regret having her at such a young age. On the other hand, having a child is a beautiful thing.

-Jacinda Rodriguez

Years

8 years old, running in the streets.
9 years old, thinking
 everybody is a cheat.
11 years old getting locked up.
12 years old, thinking I'm tough
14 years old hurting my mom's
feelings
15 years I'm out
 helping my mom with healing

-Javies Rivera

Lost One

The day you walked out of my life,
I thought I would die.
At night I would just sit in my room
and cry.
Until I had no more tears.
Why?
That's all I want to know.
Why did you have to go?
Tell me why
somebody would do this?
Somebody please tell me!
The day I lost you,
The day you were on the block
chilling with your boys,
The day you were shot.
That was the day I thought
I would die!

-Oceana Maldonado

To Me

To me, you're not just a friend,
think of everything
we've been through,
you stuck by me, I cared for you.

Those memories
weren't just memories,
you might go, but they'll never leave.
These tears aren't just tears,
they stand for all the friendship
throughout the years.

Our hood
isn't just where we grew up,
 It's where our friendship developed
 It is more than a friendship,
It goes way deep
all these memories are special to me.

-Iyana Burnett

Missing You

With the thought
of never seeing you again,
I become really tense,
Tears roll down my face,
I try not to let them know,
But they see it in my face,
They try to comfort me
& I just push them away,
But nothing can heal the way I feel,
Not medicine, Not a therapist,
Nothing can help me,
But the sound of your voice

-David Rempp

Things Change

When I was younger, I used to live in West Springfield, MA. Life was good. I went to the Boys and Girls Club after school, and my grandma would give me two dollars everyday to spend there. I was happy...until she passed away. Then I was placed in foster care because my mother had a drinking problem, and would yell at me whenever she got drunk. It was depressing, first losing Grandma, then having to live with different people. I was bouncing from place to place. I hate living in foster homes. You have to ask to get food, or to go outside.

While I was in foster care, my mom was forced to get help, or she would lose me and my sisters forever. She went to a program for 3 months. Then we lived with her at a program for a year. When the year was up, we moved to Springfield. We lived with my uncle, but then I was the one with problems in school. So, the next change was going to live with my aunt in Connecticut. While I was there, my mom started drinking again. She went back into a program . After another year, she got out, and we moved to Northampton, MA. My mom stopped drinking for a while. But only for a while.

Things continue to change for my mom and me. It makes me feel dispirited because she's not only hurting herself, but she's also hurting the ones that love her.

-Tommy W.

Daddy's Little Girl

When he said "Sweetie I'll miss you"
 I knew he would be gone
I remember Mommy saying things
But they were not true
When Mommy said "Go, Go!"
I knew she let him go
When I said "Please Mommy,
 don't let him go!"
I knew I would be alone
But I will remember
those days at the park
when he gave me a big push
 I know that my life
will never be the same
until he comes back …
 I AM DADDY"S LITTLE GIRL!!!

 -Nycole Marshall Coombs

Shannel Bell

You sang a song
 that changed my life
Your presence
 makes my days alright
Your smile
makes my world go 'round
Your voice
 is of the sweetest sound.

What you've given me
you'll never know
The love I have for you
I can never show.
You got me in touch
with the girl I am inside

The one that for many years
I tried to hide
I love me for me,
because of you
You're my role model,
the one I look up to
Now you're gone, what do I do?

Do I continue on like I never knew?
A friend like you
I never had

Now you're leaving me
 and that makes me sad
But it's okay
because our friendship will never die
I won't let it, I will fight,
sweat, and try
You're a diamond, a ruby, and a pearl
From your love I will never swirl
All my love for you,
 I can only try to tell
well here it goes...
I love you girl!!!
My one and only
                    Shannel Bell

-Ashley Hart

Sing A Song

Sing a song of despair.
The feeling of hopelessness
And loneliness,
No other feeling can compare.
Sing a song of black and white.
Opposite in separation,
Crying aloud in desperation,
Crying for her mother every night.

Sing a song of adaptation.
Where parents are unstable
And simply unable,
Adolescent frustration.

Sing a song of violation.
Unsure of whom to trust
But some relationship a must
Resulting in molestation.

Sing a song of silence.
Mouth shut in fear,
Never room for tears,

Growing up in violence.
Sing a song of responsibility.
Growing up too fast,
Never living in the past
Trying to the best of one's ability…

She knows why the caged bird
sings
Because she sang the very same
song.
She knows why the caged bird
sings
Because she was the bird all along.

- Adelia Vaughn

*"How To Live in a Box Marked
Fragile"*

*All my life
I have lived in flower stains
And in hollow egg shells,
careful not to rock
the cradle too much,
for fear the motion
will upset the quiet song inside.*

*All my life
I have lived
In the month of November,
where wanderlust and hope
burns crisp in the cool, cutting air.
Apathy always came easy,
but left hard and bitter
Realizing
it's not always the purpose of
being,
but the act of existence
that left me so drained.*

All my life
I have lived in moonbeams
and under starbursts,
* too provoked to comply,*
too underestimated
to learn how to die.

All my life
I have made love
etched in every single blue vein
Pulse through the body,
infiltrate the mind and soul,
* made sure it didn't rest*
until it erupted out of the mouth
and flew away,
free

All my life I have lived in Today,
for Yesterday pushed me away
too soon
And Tomorrow is not ready
* for the life I bring.*

All my life I have lived,
and when I live
it is not peaceful or docile-

but more like chaos and fury-
Like the eruption of flowers from
the ever repressing
Bud.

-Danusia Janiszewski

Mind of an Incarcerated Kid

I'm tired of being here,
 I'm tired of stress - filled days,
no way to get paid,
flat pockets
something I ain't used to,
girlfriends come and go,
you love them,
but then they miss you.

Days go by, loved ones die,
with no goodbyes.
But for some reason,
you're angry at them
for not waiting
until you get out.
But they don't choose the date
when their fate
ends,
you're locked kid,
come to amends.

 I pray the Lord,
thank him for the days,
 but I remember
 in the back of my mind,
 in or out,
 tomorrow
ain't promised today.
When I get out,
I'll try to make money
another way,
 but not right away,
I got to get used to it,
I'm addicted to the fast lane.
But in here, it's a school zone.

No way to get paid.
Playing Cee-Lo in a corner
For commissary
is my only hustle
 Four, five, six, yeah
 let me get that T-shirt

Claiming "Medicals"
to avoid seeing the teacher.
Being locked up is just a sign
from the man upstairs,
letting me know
 if I was *out there*,
I'd be *up there*.
 But in a week,

I'll be out there,
ready for the changes,
 seeing new faces
 But in all the same places.

                -Nate Perez

Confused

Sitting down in this dark room

thinking if I should stay

or pull this trigger and hear this loud

BOOM.

It's like I have the devil on the left

Angel on the right

And something deep down inside me

Doesn't want to win the fight

So now I'm thinking

of throwing in the towel

But life isn't that easy

If you want something

you have to go get it

But if you're confused

You let it go away

Straight up to heaven

- Dashua Lopez

Warm Heart

The day full of snow,
stranded in the mountains
where I have no where to go,
snow flakes below zero,
I'm lifeless, I need a hero.
 I'm in a state of mind
where I'm two seconds from frost bite,
so many idol in this
they seeking a lamp of false light,

I was giving up on hope
 but not quite,
let my imagination take off and take flight.
 I was seeing things
people calling my name,
as I'm lying in the snow
the cold was freezing my brain,
 rubbed my hands together, started easing
the pain, stuck in the middle of nowhere,
 polar bear came by
but I couldn't fear.
 I still had feelings

I could love,
lay straight look at the stars above.

My emotions filled with envy,
it's cold outside
what's warm within me.
 Tried to check my pulse
 I didn't know where to start,
it's cold outside plus I was in the dark,
so cold, so cold, you can't feel me apart,
the thing that kept me warm this long was
my heart.

-Jordan Malone

My Hero
(dedicated to Miss Toya aka Brenda's
Child)

Feeling alone, scared, frustrated,
All these things going through
My mind.
Is it my fault
I was entering a world of confusion,
 without being prepared?
All these things going through
My mind
Not letting it all come out...

Now I have the confidence
to face my fears,
Thanks to you, no more tears,
Now I'm anxious
to make my life happen,
Knowing I have the strength,
and the power to do what I want...

Because I'm the DIVA
 you made me.
I can finally see,
Life is what I make it,
And I'm making the most of it!

I'm not that broken stem anymore,
I'm a beautiful flower,
 because of you...I'm not a coward.
Taken me through so many things,
I finally understand, you're my hero,
and you'll always be.

It's time to let go of my hand,
and let me be free,
you've helped me,
with so many things,
 now take this and know,
 I love you, my hero

-Saphire Saez

They Call It "Puppy Love"

No matter how young,
a heart still feels,
Being a teen,
makes love naïve,
but never unreal.

<u>My Love</u>

My love surpasses
the tallest building,
Strong like water, Never breaking,
And yet it is my weakness,
It is hard like a turtle's shell,
But soft like a butterfly's wing,
This heart of mine keeps growing,
While time wears by.

- David Rempp

GONE
I didn't see it coming
you leaving me like this
  without a trace
with nothing just a lost mind
confused is the definition of lost,
 and hurt is the definition of love
Love is the definition of pain
Pain is the definition of everything

-Ebony Faison

Secret Crush

3 years ago,
I didn't notice you,
I've always thought you were cute,
but I just couldn't see,
I couldn't see us together,
Now all I want is forever.

I lied about not liking you,
and I think you like me too,
I kept it to myself for 3 years,
but this is our last year,
and it may be revealed,
up until now,
I 've kept my lips sealed.
This secret crush is no more,
I've opened the door...
I'm asking,
do you have a crush on me,
if not, just let me be.
LOL, please don't tell.

You stare at me with this look,
so why can't we be like a book,

be a fairytale

and have a happy ending,
all you'll be doing is lending…
lending your love
to someone who loves you back,
I watch that smile you crack,
and wonder if you know I like you,
because I do,
this secret crush is all about you,

So take this crush and cherish it,
because I can't deal with it,
this crush is killing inside,
my stomach feels tight,
my emotions are tied,
between telling you or not,
So much, for a secret crush,
now you know ..
I like you …very much

-Saphire Saez

Over You

Dealt with the game
for so long,
Done with the drama
that comes along
No more with rumors
No more with you

Over the arguments
Over the same dilemmas
That replay again and again

Shoot, I'm done
with the speaking!
I'm over you.

-Leslie Rivera

Fairy Tales

It's true... fairytales are just stories
no one's life is really that good.
But I can honestly say
I feel like a princess
because your doing your job,
 like every man should .

If I were Cinderella
you'd be Prince Eric
In a pile of rocks
you'd be my pearl.
Why don't you do
what Sabastian said
"Go ahead and kiss the girl."
If I'm gonna be Pocahontas
then I need a John Smith.

Your the guy that I'm dreaming of
every night
You pointed me out a new path
I've found Mr. Right.
If you haven't figured it out yet
this means I need you in my life.
Without you I'm half a heart,

half a person
I got a fork, but I need my knife

So please don't ever leave me
I'm a bee... I need a hive.
Let's prove everyone wrong
Let's make this fairytale come alive!

-Ashley Hart

Beautiful
Those crystal blue eyes,
Framed with lashes to the sky
As I gaze into them,
I see my future with you.
Soft rose colored lips
That still give me butterflies
every time they touch my skin.
Smooth sand colored skin
And big strong hands
That hold me so gently

-April Clark

Puppet

Your mischievous personality
ails my heart,
You beckon just to harass something,
Your body enthralls me,
But the words
coming from your mouth
gives me despondency,
You play with my mind
knowing I have a sensitive heart,
I try to hide it,
But I have shown too much,
You figure me out
like a reader does a book,
You begin to torment me with words
like love,
Knowing they are all lies,
All I do is sit here and cry,
For I'm the puppet
at the end of the strings,
And you're my puppeteer

-David Remmp

Inside

Bottled up inside
Are the words I never said,
The feelings that I hide
The lines you never read.
You can see it in my eyes
Read it on my face:
Trapped inside are lies
Of the past I can't replace.
With memories that linger
Won't seem to go away
Why can't I be happier?

Today's a brand new day.
Yesterdays are over,
Even though the hurting is not.
Nothing lasts forever,
I must cherish what I've got.

Don't take my love for granted
For soon it will be gone
All you ever wanted
Of the love
you'd thought you won

The hurt I'm feeling now
Won't disappear overnight,
But someway, somehow,

Everything will turn out alright

No more wishing for the past,
It wasn't meant to be.
It didn't seem to last,
So I have to set him free.

-Julia Cruz

A Lesson

While I'm thinking…
Man, I let that girl take my place,
My heart has been broken,
Shattered like a piece of glass,
We both put a lot into this relationship,
I thought we'd surely last.

You were my first true love,
My everything.
You taught me
that every swan grows a new wing.
I really did trust you from the start,
Which only left me with a damaged heart.
I thought you really loved me,
I always thought of you to be smart.

I thought you were the key to love,
Instead that key opened a door of pain,
To think I gave you me that night,
Then right after, it's another fight.
I guess I can say I've learned a lesson
One that I' ll remember
for the rest of my life.

-Shannan Swinton

You are my outlet

The one I can talk to
You are the one I write these poems for,
You're my inspiration
You are the one I live for,
My motivation
You are the one I love.

-David Rempp

Young

Wisdom

*So much has been seen
through these eyes,
time makes me young,
 but experience
 has made me wise*

"Live life to its best"

We make friends and build tradition
And everyday life is a mission
We learn to love and appreciate
The finer things in life
 we get to take
We study and educate ourselves
Middle school starts at about the age of 12

We feel the passion and the beauty of love
So beautiful, like a plain white dove
We fight and start wars
That only lead to more and more
We try to find a way to peace
But life won't make it that easy
As we grow old and the times change
It looks as if nothing changed
Like wondering where death leads to
Some place, a world, a new
The end is a destination I fear less
Than rather not living life to its best.

-Marcus Blake

Something I Just Can't Handle

The enclosed space is suffocating:
Harsh gasps, rapidly blinking eyelids,
blinding.
Body parts peel off worn leather.
I stare at the seat in front of me,
Charcoal gray, once burned.
I turn to the catalyst of my
Terror, panic; fears.
Blinders now forgotten,
I see clearly.
No longer obscured by reflecting gray
glass.
The tint –
A facade, gone, broken down.
An assortment of trash litters the street.
Drugs, violence – *death*
Taking over the city.
Homelessness increasing.
A damaged person lounging in the dying
grass
Bland, arid; stripped brown.
A gray shirt with stripes –
Endless, a long road ahead; a struggle.
Jeans faded with days past,
Matted with dirt of many shades;
A glass rainbow shattered.

Everything's broken:
Homes, families– *people.*
Legs up, ankles crossed, stomach flat
on the ground.
Thoughts of home
As he settles comfortably at a city bus
stop.
Nothing's as it was, blinders removed;
eyes opened.
Breathing returns to normal,
But the feeling in the pit of my stomach
remains.
It's too much

-Tiera Wright

Don't Call Me Kid!

Don't call me kid, I've been through it all, rent, bills, putting food in my own stomach, along with my families. Meanwhile, you're 30 years old and living in your mother's basement waiting for her to pass away so you can have her house.

When your stomach growls, what do you do? Ask "Mommy" what's for dinner? No, not me, I cook for both me and my family. I pick up after myself, and clean my own laundry…but you continue to call me a kid.

Yeah, I'm 16, in a week I'll be 17. If the law declares I can be charged as an adult, then why can't I vote? Yeah, who cares if I crack jokes or laugh at funny noises…is it my fault I have a sense of humor? My laughs don't stop me from being responsible. I have more responsibilities than half of my peers. Name another 16 or 17 year old you know paying rent, bills and buying groceries. So while you're at home sitting on your "Mommy's" sofa, sipping a cup of coffee, I'm doing what I got to do to survive. So remember one thing, I'm just as much an adult as you!

-Nate Perez

If You Feel Pain You're Still Alive

 If you feel pain you're still alive.
Is something I keep in my mind.
Go through struggles
where pain is its partner
 I say to myself...
 If you feel pain you're still alive.
Weakness takes over as I keep on striving
Close to the point where I feel like dying.
Trying to stay focused
so my body won't take over.
And I say to myself ...
If you feel pain you're still alive.

-Anthony Vega

Hidden Transformation

Trouble-making teens become future
leaders of the world.
Raging alcoholics sober up, soak up the
world.
Appreciative parents await the birth of a
daughter.
Nations are destroyed by the lack of
drinking water.
Small children grow up as products of
environment,
Forever disappointing society's
requirements.
Oblivious businesses are ripped off by the
act of robbery.
Rewarding the sinner trying to combat a life
of poverty.
Mexicans cross the border for a chance at a
better life.
Americans conceal insecurities, resorting to
the surgical knife.
Turmoil-causing gang members act hard,
never smile.
Individuals ain't so tough on the stand,
awaiting trial.
Others criticize, force an opinion change.
Never will I believe, anything stays the
same.

                    -Martin Payne

Crazy Girl World

It's 6:00 AM
And I can't sleep.
In thoughts, I am way too deep.
I'm thinking about all the secrets and
promises
 I've sworn to keep.
I've got to balance all these different
personalities
Around each one of my posses,
I can't just let loose
And be the real me.

I can't say who I like,
I can't tell her who she loves,
I can't reveal what she said,
Or who she's dreaming of.
I can't give a hint to how she really feels
 about her shoes,
How she thinks she's shallow,
Or how she's got the blues.
'Cause she thinks her man's cheating on her
With that flirty blonde,
Who's supposed to be her Best Friend.

Can't tell that the red head talks
'bout the Prom Queen,
Though they're sisters, who perfectly blend.
The brunette talks about the gossiper behind her back,
Says class is what she lacks.
Though I agree,
I say nothing, to no one
In this teenage girl world,
Gossip can kill.
Keeping quiet is a very rare skill.
Keep all opinions to yourself –
Don't leave your feelings open on a shelf.
Don't let yourself be sucked in,
'Cause then there's no way you can win.
Honesty isn't always the best policy,
But loyalty is the best quality.
Choose your words wisely,
Hear the truth slyly:
Watch your mouth in this *crazy girl world*

-Hanna McGeed

Following was inspired by and includes quotes
Toni Morrison's "Beloved" and Maya Angelou's
"Still I Rise"

A Mother's Love is Great

"You may write me down in history
With your bitter, twisted lies,
You may trod me in the very dirt,
But still, like dust, I'll rise."

Sethe was a mother. She was a *Black*
mother. Her babies didn't belong to her, they
belonged to Schoolteacher. She had to fight.
She had to win. She had to escape. She took
her babies, all four of them, and did what no
one believed was possible. Risking death in
the face of failure, she fled Sweet Home,
dragging two young boys behind her, and
clutching two baby girls to her breast. A
mother's love is great. But they found her. It
didn't matter how far she went, or how long
she was gone. Twenty-eight days of
freedom, and then they came. She had to
save them, and she did. She saved them all.

A mother's love is great. "They ain't with Schoolteacher. They ain't at Sweet Home." They're safe, but at what cost?

"Animal."
Eighteen years later, only one remains "safe". One is dead, killed by her own hand, and two are missing, driven off by the vengeful spirit that remained. "You got two feet, Sethe, not four." Why did you do it? You could have waited, been patient, and bought their freedom. A mother's love is great. You don't understand. You didn't carry my babies inside yourself for nine months each! I am theirs and they are mine. I did what I had to. A mother's love is great.

"Did you want to see me broken?"

They took her son, they drove her daughter-in-law to the brink of insanity, and they killed her granddaughter. Baby Suggs should have had a lot more than just bitterness towards her slave-owners, but she didn't. A wise woman, a preacher, and she knew how the world worked. Give birth to your children, and less than a fortnight later, you won't see them again. "What was left to hurt her?" A mother's love is great. What is the greatest insult one could bestow upon a woman? To deprive her of God's greatest gift: motherhood. "Four girls, and the last time she saw them there was no hair under their arms… what would be the point of looking at the youngest one too hard?" A mother's love is great. What evil could be malignant enough to break that?

"Animal."
"I don't have to tell you about Sweet Home- what it was- but maybe you don't know that it was like for me to get away from there." They called me an animal for protecting my children, and were disgusted by my actions. If you don't want me to be an animal, take off my chains and stop treating me like your dog. I did what I had to do. A mother's love is great, but she needs to be able to love. "I couldn't love 'em proper in Kentucky because they weren't mine to love." You took my ability to love away from me. So, who *truly* is the animal?

"You may cut me with your eyes."

A mother's love is great. So great, in fact, that it can overpower sanity. Denver loves her mother, but she knows that her love runs thick, too thick. "Love is or it ain't. Thin love ain't love at all." But thick love can kill, and rumors run deep, passed on through generation after generation. A mother's love is great. She took a handsaw to her own children. "Didn't your mother get locked away for murder? Wasn't you in there with her when she went?" Twenty-eight days of joy, and then they came. "A pretty little slave girl recognized a hat, and then split to the woodshed to kill her children."

"Animal."

"Beloved is my sister. I swallowed her blood right along with my mother's milk." I was saved, but I was condemned to live my life of freedom in solitude. I never got a choice. I was never asked. I don't know what it was, and I may never know, but whatever it was that made my mother kill one of her own daughters, it came from outside. It could come back. I don't want to die, so I have to stay here, and watch, to make sure my mother doesn't have to kill me too. A mother's love is great, but it has left me with nothing. I have no friends, my family has left me, and my mother may kill me. Beloved is all I have left. "She's mine, Beloved. She's mine."

"You may kill me with your hatefulness."
Beloved was two years old when her mother slit her throat. She loved her. She saved her. She killed her. But her love was tough, and Beloved came back. A mother's love is great. She took her, and put her in a place where she would be safe. She *killed* her. *You* killed her. "I'll tend her as no mother ever tended a child, a daughter." Your love ain't safe. "My plan was to take us all to the other side, where my own ma'am is. They stopped me from getting us there." My love freed her. She was safe. She was dead.

"Animal."
"I am Beloved and she is mine." Sethe is my mother. I am her greatest thing. She love me, and I have to have her. She killed me, but I came back. A mother's love is great. Paul D tried to run me off. "Who in the world is he willing to die for?" I am yours and you are mine. In the end, we are together, and that is all that matters.

"I am the dream and the hope of the slave."
"I am the dream and the hope of the slave."

We are free. We were threatened, we were beaten. Our milk was stolen, and we were killed. But, we are free. You may look down on us and call us animals. You may claim that we are beneath you and because of that, claim you have a right to own us, but we beat you. A mother's love is great and it protects us. We are free.

"I rise

I rise

I rise."

- Rebecca Davis

The following was inspired by the JENA SIX and the "White" tree in Louisiana.

TRICK OR TREED:

A. Tree's Perspective
Oak, maple, apple, and pear? We come in many shapes, sizes and types. For years, we've been abused, and yet we stayed silent. But no more!
My fellow peers and I have evolved much. It has always been said that silence speaks a thousand words, now the Trees do. We use to mark changes in seasons, now, we've been lessened to racial crimes. I'm sure everyone has seen the latest headlines, apparently we Trees HAVE RACES! So much so that violence ensued. Who knew racial crimes would involve a Tree?
Plus, what's the deal with all these horrible clichés and bad jokes? *The apple doesn't fall far from the tree;* used and abused, next! *Make like a tree and leave* (Drum roll anyone). I'm just so insulted. I don't get how we Trees became one big joke. I'm literally stumped. What happened to the times when we were treated like a work of beauty? Living in a peaceful state where

we were the apple of an artist or poet's eye. What happened to the days when parents would hang up a swing for their children's entertainment, instead of the hanging of nooses to degrade the races of others? What happened to the days when people could sit under my wing for shade? What happened to the days where I used to house birds, bees, Pooh and Tigger too? What happened to the days when people wanted to save the environment, themselves, and us? Now no one has respect for anyone, and what's sad is they don't even have any respect for themselves either.

I think we've been through enough; if it's not paper, it's racism. Why can't we be left alone? There may be no "I" in TEAM, but there is a Tree in RESPECT.

Article by A. Tree

-Tiera Wright

"Life is Part of the Struggle"

Being poor must be like fate
'Cause all these rich people act so
fake
Smoking cigarettes must be fun
About as cheap as a toy gun
Hitting a girl must make you strong
'Cause you never think you doing
wrong

Going to school isn't cool anymore
 Brothas would rather just work at
the stores
Getting pregnant is a big deal
Like a permanent scare that will
never heal

Being in gangs is the way of life
Watch as young kids become the
center of strife
How going to jail isn't like on TV
It's a lot more harder than it really
seems

Like parents being strict
on fresh kids
On every little bad thing they did
Like when you mom cries at night
alone
And your sitting here reading this
poem
Life isn't easy for **anyone** these
days
It's struggle… just finding a way

-Marcus Blake

In a Streets

In the streets, I see fiends,
 waiting for that next rock.
It's a cool, calm, windy day,
And it feels a little hot.
The streets are grimy,
they need fixing up
They need to hit the strip up,
With a cement truck.
The smell is really crazy,
This downtown air.
The pollution is really nasty,
And it's not fair.
I hear birds chirping,
At least, they are living right
They got more freedom than me,
So I guess it's alright.

- Jerel Brunson

Miss Toya's Testimony

My mother died six months before my fifth birthday. I was fortunate enough as a child not to feel her absence because of my maternal grandmother. My "Ga-Ga," as we affectionately called her, took responsibility for my sister and me after her twenty-three year old daughter succumbed to breast cancer. Ga-Ga became my mother and my best friend.

On Christmas Day of 1991,Ga-Ga lost her battle with ovarian cancer. She was 58. I was 13 and traumatized. I still had five aunts in my life who stepped up to care for my sister and me, but losing Ga-Ga left me with a void in my heart and a broken spirit. Each Mother's Day following Ga-Ga's death, I smiled while attending church and family dinners. Inside, I was hurt and bewildered. But I could never share this with my family because I didn't want to make anyone else as sad as I was; besides I was supposed to be the "strong one" who never cried.

I felt I had no purpose. I had no desire. Like a programmed robot, I systemically marched through my adolescent years: school, work and home. I made the honor roll, I participated in after-school activities, and hung out with friends. To the outside world, I was your average high school student. But inside, I was desolate, a candle whose flame had been blown out. I did things because I was expected to do them, not because I wanted to.

Then in my senior year, the FIRE in me was re ignited by my Psychology/ African-American History teacher, Carol Hoffman. She saw something in me that I didn't see in myself. This teacher made me *want* to learn again and she made me feel special. To this day, I'm still not sure what it is about that woman that made me feel good inside, that compelled me to reach for goals for *myself* and not just for others. Whatever it was, I'm thankful for it.

While I was in college, I wrote Mrs. Hoffman (who had become Mrs. Sullivan) a letter telling her how influential she was to me. She had no idea that she'd made so much of an impact on my life in such a short period of time. That's the thing about working with young people…sometimes you never know how much your time, love and support means to them until later.

Miss Toya's Bio

Miss Toya, as she is called by all of "Her Kids" is a special education teacher for the Springfield, Massachusetts Public Schools. She has myriad of Human Service experience, particularly with at-risk youth and families. Over the last ten years, She has worked in programs affiliated with the Department of Social Services, and Department of Youth Services. She has also implemented curriculum for after school programs and summer camps. Miss Toya has made a lifetime commitment to inspire youth.

In 2006, Miss Toya established her own youth program, Keep Youth Dreaming and Striving (KYDS), aimed at promoting self-esteem and providing youth with a sense of purpose. For more information visit: www.keepyouthdreamingandstriving.com

BIOS

Born Latoya Bosworth, she dubbed herself Brenda's Child at the age of 21, in honor of her late mother Brenda Kay Swinton.

But really.. who is she?

Brenda's Child is the confident diva, with a smooth spoken word style. She has been writing poetry for 15 years, and performing spoken word for 6 years. She uses her poetry as an outlet as she experiences the daily joys and struggles of being a mother, youth advocate, teacher, African-American, female, optimist, and dream seeker.

Brenda's Child loves to write poetry that is uplifting and inspiring. Brenda's Child emphasizes self-love, worth, and value. She also feels obligated to tell the truth... even if it hurts.

Brenda's Child's poetry is currently featured in the Pen&Ink column of the community newspaper Springfield, Massachusetts based.

"An African-American Point of View" .

In April of 2007 Brenda's Child self-published her first book of poetry entitled *"A Piece of My Mind...Poetic Confessions of a Self-Proclaimed Diva"*

For more information contact : brendaschild@brendaschild.com

THE WRITERS

Annamarie Alleyne-Lovell attends Springfield Central High School. She aspires to become a Neurological surgeon and wishes to continue writing on the side, since writers block will have her homeless on the *block* during sporadic months of the year.

Marcus Blake

Jerel Brunson has dreams of being a chef or an veterinarian. His biggest goal is to make something of his life and stay off of the streets. He was a student of Miss Toya's, and his poem was originally an assignment.

Iyana Burnett loves to model, write music and sing. She believes that if you are confident, you can do anything. She is a member of Miss Toya's youth program, KYDS.

Angela Bessey is a graduate of Holyoke High School. She enjoys going to the gym, listening to music, doing art, and hanging out with her friends. She plans to attend Holyoke Community College and major in Liberal Arts.

April Clark was born and raised by in Springfield, MA. She aspires to be a kindergarten teacher. April enjoys cheerleading, playing soccer, and writing poetry. April has also been a student of Miss Toya.

Maria Colon likes to write her emotions down as poetry. She has struggled throughout life, and is now headed for success. Miss Toya has worked with Maria in educational and recreational settings since she was 10 years old.

Julia Cruz is a student at New Leadership Charter School in Springfield, MA. She loves to write in her spare time.

Rebecca Davis has been writing since she learned how to hold a pen and plans to continue for quite awhile. She also plays basketball and piano and is looking forward to attending Northeastern University in the Fall of 2008.

Ebony Faison loves to dance. She loves enjoys discussing current events and how they affect human lives. She is a member of KYDS.

Ashley Hart is a 17 year old student at Springfield Central High School in Massachusetts. In continuing with family tradition, she is a cousin of Miss Toya.

Danusia Janiszewki is an 18 year old dreamer who has finished her public education at Springfield Central High and is attending Mt. Holyoke in the autumn. Her ambitions, though yet not yet sculpted, are boundless and intended for global revolution.

Dashua Lopez lives in Springfield, MA. He strongly believes that if you have a dream, you should never give up.

Oceana Maldonado is an 18 year old senior in high school. Her poem is about one of her friends who was killed on April 20, 2007 due to gang violence.

Jordan Malone's poetry has been recognized nationally. He recently began reciting poetry at local poetry venues in Springfield, MA.

Nycole Marshall-Combs, is attends Springfield Academy for Excellence in Massachusetts. In her spare time, she likes to listen to music and write poetry.

Hannah McGeed attends Holy Cross School in Massachusetts. She has been writing poetry since she was in second grade - starting with little kid rhymes, which eventually grew into multiple-page poems. She has notebooks full of poetry and hopes to see more of it published. She would like to thank her friends and family who inspire her work and encourage her to keep writing.

Ricardo Navarro loves to write rhymes and feels he's destined to be a star one day, despite his past mistakes. Ricardo has been a student of Miss Toya.

Martin Payne is 17 years old and attends Cathedral High School in Massachusetts. He is a brother to three siblings.

Nate Perez wants to become a barber. He loves to tell stories about his life. He has been a student of Miss Toya.

David Rempp is a 16 year old student at Springfield Academy For Excellence in Springfield, Massachusetts.

Javies Rivera aspires to be an interpreter for the deaf. Javies has been a student of Miss Toya, and is a member of KYDS.

Leslie Rivera

Jacinda Lee Rodriguez is a student at Springfield Academy For Excellence in Springfield, Massachusetts. She is looking forward to graduating high school, and going to college to study nursing. Aside from school Jacinda enjoys also enjoy doing hair, and spending time with friends.

Saphire Saez attends Springfield Central high school. She aspires to be like Miss Toya (Brenda's Child) by mentoring youth and having her own youth program. Saphire is an original member and youth assistant for KYDS.

Lorianna Stephens is a student at The High School of Science and Technology in Springfield, Massachusetts. She loves to write and perform spoken word poetry. Lorianna is a member of KYDS.

Shannan Swinton is a graduate of Sabbis International Charter School. She likes fashion, and writing poetry. She is a cousin to Miss Toya.

Adelia Vaughn is a 17 year old resident of Springfield, MA. Her poem was chosen from her entry in the Springfield Public Library Poetry Contest.

Anthony Vega, is 17 years old and lives in Holyoke Ma. He attends school at Holyoke High School.

Tommy W. like sports and meeting new people. Tommy has been a student of Miss Toya, and is also a KYDS member.

Tiera Wright, is a graduate of Springfield Central High School in Massachusetts. She plans to major in Liberal Studies at Bay Path College and have a professional career in writing, with a focus on Poetry and Short Stories.

www.ingramcontent.com/pod-product-compliance
Lightning Source LLC
Chambersburg PA
CBHW032015040426
42448CB00006B/640